I0644375

# Tubas Contents

Buzz, buzz. Push the valves.
Get ready to play the tuba!

The tuba is a wind instrument. It makes very low sounds. A tuba has valves. Pressing a valve changes the tuba's sound.

Tubas have three to six valves.

8

A tuba is a heavy instrument. Tuba players usually sit down to play. They hold the tuba across their lap.

Tuba players flap their lips.
They press them on the
tuba's mouthpiece.
This makes a sound.

Marching bands use special tubas. They are called sousaphones. Sousaphones are easier for people to carry than normal tubas.

A tuba is made from a long metal tube that curves around. The tube can be as long as three people.

The first tubas were made of wood. They looked like snakes. Modern tubas were invented about 200 years ago.

**The first tuba was made in Germany.**

Tubas are used in jazz music. People also play them in orchestras. There is usually only one tuba in an orchestra.

In 2006, a woman played the tuba in a major orchestra for the first time.

People can play tubas together in a group. A tuba quartet is a group of four tubas. The largest group of tubas had 835 players.

clash
PUNK
speaker

See what you have learned about tubas.

Which of these pictures does not show a tuba?

# KEY WORDS

Research has shown that as much as 65 percent of all written material published in English is made up of 300 words. These 300 words cannot be taught using pictures or learned by sounding them out. They must be recognized by sight. This book contains 52 common sight words to help young readers improve their reading fluency and comprehension. This book also teaches young readers several important content words, such as proper nouns. These words are paired with pictures to aid in learning and improve understanding.

| Page | Sight Words First Appearance |
|---|---|
| 5 | get, play, the, to |
| 6 | a, changes, has, have, is, it, makes, sounds, three, very |
| 9 | down, their, they |
| 11 | on, them, this |
| 12 | are, carry, for, people, than, use |
| 15 | around, as, be, can, from, long, made, that |
| 16 | about, first, in, like, of, was, were, years |
| 19 | also, an, one, only, there, time |
| 20 | four, group, had, together |

| Page | Content Words First Appearance |
|---|---|
| 5 | tuba, valves |
| 6 | wind instrument |
| 9 | lap, players |
| 11 | lips, mouthpiece |
| 12 | marching bands, sousaphones |
| 15 | tube |
| 16 | Germany, snakes, wood |
| 19 | jazz music, orchestras, woman |
| 20 | quartet |

Published by AV2
350 5th Avenue, 59th Floor New York, NY 10118
Website: www.av2books.com

Copyright ©2021 AV2
All rights reserved. No part of this publication may be reproduced, stored in a retrieval system, or transmitted in any form or by any means, electronic, mechanical, photocopying, recording, or otherwise, without the prior written permission of the publisher.

Library of Congress Cataloging-in-Publication Data

Names: Daly, Ruth, 1962- author.
Title: Tubas / Ruth Daly.
Description: New York : AV2, 2020. | Series: Musical instruments |
Audience: Ages 6-9 | Audience: Grades K-1 |
Identifiers: LCCN 2019042734 (print) | LCCN 2019042735 (ebook) | ISBN 9781791116163 (library binding) |
ISBN 9781791116170 (paperback) | ISBN 9781791116187 | ISBN 9781791116194
Subjects: LCSH: Tuba--Juvenile literature.

Classification: LCC ML970 .D35 2020 (print) | LCC ML970 (ebook) | DDC 788.9/819--dc23
LC record available at https://lccn.loc.gov/2019042734
LC ebook record available at https://lccn.loc.gov/2019042735

Printed in Guangzhou, China
1 2 3 4 5 6 7 8 9 0 24 23 22 21 20

022020
100919

Project Coordinator: John Willis Designer: Ana María Vidal

The publisher acknowledges Alamy, Bridgeman Images, Getty Images, iStock, and Shutterstock as the primary image suppliers for this title.